§sas. | SAS Publishing

Annotate:
ART CARPENTER'S SAS® SOFTWARE SERIES
Simply the Basics

Art Carpenter

The Power to Know®

The correct bibliographic citation for this manual is as follows: Carpenter, Art. 1999. *Annotate: Simply the Basics.* Cary, NC: SAS Institute Inc.

Annotate: Simply the Basics

Copyright © 1999 by SAS Institute Inc., Cary, NC, USA

ISBN 1-58025-578-7

SAS Institute Inc., SAS Campus Drive, Cary, North Carolina 27513.

1st printing, October 1999
2nd printing, February 2000
3rd printing, June 2002
4th printing, March 2003

SAS Publishing provides a complete selection of books and electronic products to help customers use SAS software to its fullest potential. For more information about our e-books, e-learning products, CDs, and hard-copy books, visit the SAS Publishing Web site at **support.sas.com/pubs** or call 1-800-727-3228.

Table of Contents

Foreword by the Series Editor

Art Carpenter

This is the first work in what will be an ongoing series of titles. We will provide short and narrowly focused topics on subjects that you will be able to put to immediate use. Do you want practical information with lots of examples? This series will be a great source of useful code and timely information.

Shorter than a reference book but longer than a SUGI paper, this series offers authors an excellent medium for covering a specific topic in real detail. If you have a topic that you would like to write on, contact SAS Institute's Books By Users Program at sasbbu@sas.com.

Preface

For many users of SAS/GRAPH software, the learning curve for the Annotate facility seems to be quite steep. This monograph provides a simple introduction to the power and simplicity of the Annotate facility. This text is a synthesis of several papers and workshops that have been presented at SUGI conferences. It also borrows from the author's three-day course on SAS/GRAPH.

Only a few brief aspects of the Annotate facility are covered in this text. The intent is not to provide an alternative to the reference manuals, but rather to provide what the manuals do not – a simple way for you to get started using Annotate. This monograph will show you how to take baby steps. Try it out, and soon you will be running your own races!

Acknowledgments

I would like to express my appreciation to Dee Doles, Patsy Poole, Julie Platt, and Hanna Schoenrock of the Books By Users Program at SAS Institute for coordinating and editing this project. Special thanks are also extended to Richard O. Smith for reviewing the draft manuscript.

The data used in this book is fictional and does not reflect any actual industries or business ventures of actual industrial tycoons.

Using This Book

This monograph was written to be read linearly by a reader unfamiliar with the structure and usage of the Annotate facility. The reader should have a working knowledge of basic SAS/GRAPH procedures and the DATA step.

The first two chapters introduce the Annotate data set and the features that make it unique within the SAS System. These chapters also provide a strategy for creating Annotate data sets that will ultimately accomplish your goals. This introduction concludes in Chapter 3, which demonstrates the use of very simple Annotate examples.

Chapter 4 discusses the building of Annotate data sets. These can be based on flat files, other SAS data sets, and assignment statements from within a DATA step. Examples show the key elements for these data sets and alternative statement structures.

Most users want to be able to use Annotate to enhance the output of standard procedures within SAS/GRAPH. Chapter 5 introduces the topic by showing examples that add labels and text to both scatter plots and histograms.

The final chapter, Chapter 6, is really an introduction to an advanced topic within Annotate. A number of SAS macros have been written to make it easier to create Annotate data sets. This chapter introduces the use of Annotate macros.

Throughout the book references are made to other sources of information. **See Also** is used to point to other sections within this monograph that contain additional information on the topic. Also, a great deal of information is contained in the literature. The heading **More Information** is used to indicate sources (including reference manuals and SUGI papers) that contain information related to the current section.

CHAPTER 1

Introduction to the Annotate Facility

1.1 Chapter Overview

The Annotate facility allows the user to create customized modifications to the graphic output. These modifications can be either predetermined or data driven. This means that, through the use of Annotate, you can greatly extend the already powerful capabilities of SAS/GRAPH.

This chapter introduces the basic concepts associated with the Annotate facility and gives you some background into how we will use Annotate to communicate with the SAS/GRAPH procedures used to produce graphs and charts. If you already have an initial understanding of the concept of the Annotate data set, you may skip this chapter.

You may use Annotate with the following SAS/GRAPH procedures:

GANNO   displays the output from Annotate data sets.

GCHART   produces histograms and charts.

GCONTOUR   creates contour plots.

GMAP   uses coordinate data sets to produce maps.

GPLOT   produces scatter plots.

GPRINT   displays printed output.

GSLIDE   creates panels that primarily contain textual information.

G3D   creates three-dimensional plots.

Many users of SAS/GRAPH have avoided using Annotate because of what they perceive to be a rather steep and long learning curve. This is an unfortunate misconception. Using Annotate need not be difficult and can be easily introduced by presenting the different fundamentals of the specialized Annotate data set.

1.2   What Is the Annotate Facility?

The Annotate facility is included within SAS/GRAPH and acts as a bridge between the procedure selected by the user and the user's desire to customize the graphics output.

The Annotate Facility can be used to

- position text or symbols anywhere on the graph

- control text color, font, and size

- draw line segments of any length or thickness

- draw polygons of any style, size, or shape

- otherwise enhance your graph.

The power of the Annotate facility is accessed through the use of a specialized data set. When using this data set Annotate looks for variables with specific names and attributes, and the values taken on by these variables let Annotate know what your intentions are.

1.3   Annotate Data Set

The Annotate data set is an ordinary SAS data set. It in no way differs from any other SAS data set. Unlike most SAS data sets, however, the Annotate data set is more rigidly defined in terms of the variables that it is to contain and the attributes that these variables must have.

Although the construction of Annotate data sets is often viewed as a daunting task for users who are unfamiliar with the way SAS/GRAPH assimilates the Annotate commands, the Annotate data set can actually be created in any of the ways that any SAS data set is created. Usually a DATA step is used with one of the following techniques:

- Small control data sets can be created using assignment statements.

- Flat files or raw data can be read into an Annotate data set.

- Existing SAS data sets can be restructured into Annotate data sets.

Although at first it seems clumsy to pass specific information to a procedure through the use of dedicated data sets, procedures are designed to accept, interpret, and respond to SAS data sets. Therefore, an Annotate data set can contain the functional information and procedure statements that could not be included in the PROC step itself. The result is a stronger and more flexible approach.

More Information

SAS/GRAPH Software: Usage, Version 6, Chapter 54 provides a good overview of the Annotate data set as well as several important Annotate variables.

Version 7 and 8 users should consult *SAS OnlineDoc.*

1.3.1 *Structure of the Annotate data set*

The SAS/GRAPH procedures sequentially read the observations from the Annotate data set and search for specific variables. The values taken on by these variables direct the Annotate facility to perform the desired actions.

Each observation requests that Annotate perform a particular function. The requested function causes Annotate to look for those variables that can be used to modify that particular function. Other variables that do not relate to that function for that Annotate observation are ignored.

1.3.2 *Types of Annotate variables*

An Annotate data set can contain over 20 variables that have specific meanings. Fortunately, the new user need not master all of them prior to creating an annotated plot or graph. Basically, three questions need to be answered. What to do? How to do it? Where to do it?

The three primary Annotate variables, **FUNCTION**, **X**, and **Y**, are needed for most Annotate observations. FUNCTION tells Annotate *what to do,* and X and Y tell Annotate *where to do it.* Most of the other Annotate variables are used to enhance or supplement these three by providing information on *how to do it.*

1.3.3 *Using variables to control tasks*

Because the Annotate data set is processed one observation at a time, the value of the variable FUNCTION is evaluated for each observation. The value that FUNCTION takes on determines which of the other variables in the observation may have information applicable to the FUNCTION and, therefore, to the observation being processed. The action specified by the FUNCTION, along with whatever modifiers are appropriate, takes place before the next observation is read.

WHAT	WHERE	HOW
FUNCTION	X Y XSYS YSYS	POSITION SIZE STYLE LINE TEXT
LABEL	* * * *	* * * *
MOVE	* * * *	
DRAW	* * * *	* *

Table 1.3.3 *Selected Annotate variables and whether they are used when FUNCTION is equal to LABEL, MOVE, or DRAW*

Table 1.3.3 shows several typical Annotate variables and whether they are used (indicated with an asterisk) with various values of the FUNCTION variable. Shown are three possible values of the variable FUNCTION ('LABEL', 'MOVE', and 'DRAW'). On an observation that has FUNCTION='DRAW', for instance, the variables SIZE and LINE will be used when defined. However, when an observation has FUNCTION='MOVE', the variables SIZE and LINE will be ignored.

Some of the supporting variables convey different information to Annotate depending on the value of the variable FUNCTION. When FUNCTION='LABEL', the variable SIZE refers to the height of the text to be printed, but when FUNCTION='DRAW', SIZE relates to the width of the line to be drawn.

The construction of the data set is fairly straightforward as long as you start with the definition of the FUNCTION for each observation in the Annotate data set. The selected FUNCTION determines what other variables will be needed. After you select the value of FUNCTION and appropriate support variables, the coordinates (X and Y) need to be supplied. These coordinates may be in the units of the plotted data or in units that define the graphics window itself. You will need to use the variables XSYS and YSYS to help set up the coordinate system for X and Y.

See Also

Section 2.4 provides more detailed information about the values taken on by XSYS and YSYS.

More Information

SAS/GRAPH Software: Usage, Version 6, pp. 754—755 contains additional information on the coordinate systems and using XSYS and YSYS.

Version 7 and 8 users should consult *SAS OnlineDoc*.

CHAPTER 2

The Annotate Process
(What, How, Where)

2.1   Chapter Overview

Because Annotate is used primarily to enhance a graph, the first step for the programmer faced with using the Annotate facility is to determine what needs to be done. The answer will usually take the form of something like "add a label", "include a legend in the upper right corner", or "draw a triangle." This information is passed to Annotate through specific variables in the Annotate data set. It is very important for you to remember that specific variables are used to answer the following questions:

- **What** is to be done?

- **How** is it to be done?

- **Where** is it to be done?

The variables that you use in the Annotate data set pass **all** of the information to the   graphics procedure.   Just as in gourmet cooking, where "the presentation is everything," in Annotate, variable selection is everything. The variable FUNCTION, for the most part, dictates what other variables will be needed and used.

Once the FUNCTION (**what**) has been determined, its supporting variables (**how**) and the location variables (**where**) are determined.

This process can be summarized as

1. Select a FUNCTION (**what**).

2. Select support variables (**how**) such as SIZE, COLOR, and STYLE.

3. Select coordinate system and coordinate variables (**where**).

4. Assign values to the Annotate variables for each observation in the Annotate data set.

THIS CHAPTER'S SECTION	SAS/GRAPH REFERENCE PAGES	ANNOTATE TOPIC
2.2	pp. 536-569	WHAT – Selection of Functions and associated variables.
2.3	pp. 513-534	HOW – Annotate variables and the functions with which they are used.
2.4		WHERE – Location variables are detailed as Annotate variables.

Table 2.1   *Each of the remaining sections in this chapter correspond to WHAT, HOW, and WHERE*

More Information

The primary SAS reference for determining syntax and which variables go with what functions is Chapter 19 *in SAS/GRAPH Software: Reference, Version 6, Volume 1*, pp. 513–596. This chapter is organized into several sections, and two of these sections correspond to Sections 2.2 and 2.3.

A short overview of this process is discussed by Gilbert, 1999.

Version 7 and 8 users should consult *SAS OnlineDoc*.

2.2 WHAT - Control through the Variable FUNCTION

The character variable FUNCTION provides the information on WHAT is to be done. Virtually all Annotate data sets will have this variable defined for all observations.   Because FUNCTION provides the user with the ability to express what is to be done, it is one of the best places for you to start when creating an Annotate data set.

Some of the Annotate functions include

BAR   creates a fillable rectangle.

DRAW   draws a line.

LABEL   places text or symbols on the graphic.

MOVE   allows movement to a specific point on the graphic.

PIE   creates a fillable slice, arc, or circle.

POINT   places a single point.

POLY   starts the creation of a polygon.

POLYCONT   continues the creation of a polygon.

SYMBOL   places a symbol on the graphic.

See Also

The functions LABEL, MOVE, and DRAW are discussed in more detail in Section 2.3.

More Information

Gilbert, 1999, pp. 1002–1005. This SUGI paper shows how to customize SAS graphs using the Annotate facility and global statements.

SAS/GRAPH Software: Reference, Version 6, Volume 1, pp. 472–473, Table 18.1, lists the Annotate variables and Table 18.2, p.474 lists the FUNCTION values.

SAS/GRAPH Software: Reference, Version 6, Volume 1, pp. 513–596, Chapter 19, provides a dictionary of all of the functions and associated variables and their syntax.

2.3 HOW - Attribute Variables

The process of selecting the variables to include in the Annotate data set should **always** start with FUNCTION. The value of the FUNCTION variable will determine what other variables are needed. These supporting attribute variables might include font selection (STYLE), size of the text (SIZE), and color of text (COLOR).

The concept of attribute variables is demonstrated below for the LABEL, MOVE, and DRAW functions. As you read about these three functions, notice that different attribute variables are applied to each value of FUNCTION. Indeed at times a particular attribute variable, for example SIZE, will have different meanings for different values of FUNCTION.

FUNCTION='LABEL'

A label consisting of a symbol, character, or text string is added to a plot when FUNCTION='LABEL'. This alerts Annotate that a text string (contained in the variable TEXT) is to be placed on the graph. Other variables are available to enhance the text's color (COLOR), size (SIZE), and font (STYLE) [see Table 1.3.3].

Some of the variables used with FUNCTION='LABEL' include

TEXT='*string*'   add *string* to display

COLOR='*color*'   specify the color of text

SIZE=*n*   specify size of text

STYLE='*font*'   select font for text string.

The attributes of TEXT are controlled in a similar fashion as they are in a SAS/GRAPH TITLE or FOOTNOTE statement. The size of the text is controlled by the SIZE variable in much the same way as height (H=) is used in a TITLE statement. Font selection is controlled through the STYLE variable that corresponds to the font option (F=). The variable COLOR specifies the color as does color option (C=) in titles and footnotes.

FUNCTION='MOVE' and FUNCTION='DRAW'

FUNCTION='MOVE' picks up and moves the pen (this may be an imaginary or virtual pen on many hardcopy devices, such as plotters, and on display windows) to a specified location. When a FUNCTION='MOVE' is followed by a FUNCTION='DRAW', a line is drawn from the location specified by the MOVE to the location specified by the DRAW. By using a series of MOVEs and DRAWs you can sketch a simple to complex diagram. When drawing (using FUNCTION= DRAW), the variable LINE specifies the style of the line (solid, dashed, and so on). The line thickness may also be controlled through the use of SIZE.

Variables used when FUNCTION='DRAW' include

COLOR=*'color'*   color of the line

LINE=*n*   type of line to draw (uses the same line definitions as the SYMBOL statement)

SIZE=*n*   width of the line.

2.4 WHERE - Positioning Variables

For nearly all of the values of FUNCTION, the location on the graph must be selected, that is **where** on the graph should the annotation be placed. The coordinates are usually placed using the numeric variables X and Y. How these coordinates are interpreted depends on the coordinate system, which is specified by the XSYS and YSYS variables. These variables may be defined explicitly in a DATA step or their values may be data driven. In either case, X is used to define horizontal coordinates and Y the vertical coordinates.

The physical location on the graph depends on the coordinate system, which can be selected by using the character variables XSYS and YSYS. Although these variables can take on one of twelve "system" values, three of these values for XSYS and YSYS will satisfy most of your Annotate needs.

Where a particular value of X will be located depends on the value assigned to XSYS. When XSYS='3' (graphics output area percentage), a value of X=50 will be plotted in the middle of the page. However, when XSYS='2' (data value), the placement depends on the horizontal axis on the plot or graph. For instance, if the axis ranges from 0 to 55, X=50 will be located on the far right of this axis area.

The values of XSYS and YSYS need not be constant in the Annotate data set. As a matter of fact, for a given observation, XSYS and YSYS do not even need to have the same values.

XSYS & YSYS='2'   'Absolute data area' places the point according to the values of the horizontal and vertical axes that are plotted on the graph (Figure 2.4a).

XSYS & YSYS='3'   'Absolute graphics output area percent' uses percentages of the entire graphics area, which are measured from the lower left corner (Figure 2.4b).

XSYS & YSYS='5'   'Absolute procedure output area percent' uses percentages of the entire graphics area, excluding any space taken by titles and footnotes.   The percentages are measured from the lower left corner (Figure 2.4c).

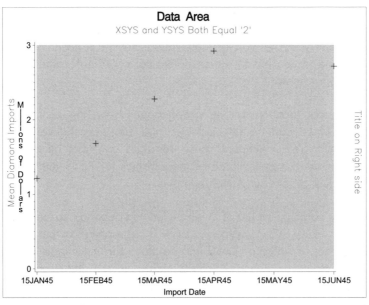

Figure 2.4a *Area accessible using the absolute data value coordinate system*

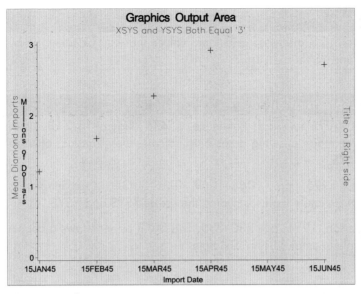

Figure 2.4b *Area accessible using the absolute graphics output area percent coordinate system*

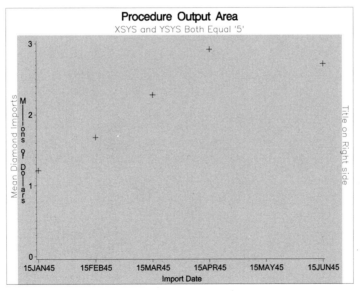

Figure 2.4c *Area accessible using the absolute procedure output area percent coordinate system*

See Also

Section 5.4.3 discusses additional values that can be taken on by XSYS and YSYS.

More Information

SAS/GRAPH Software: Reference, p 476. Figure 18.2 discusses the three major drawing areas and indicates the 12 values of XSYS and YSYS.

Griffin, 1995, pp. 1064–1069. This SUGI paper introduces several Annotate topics including the use of XSYS and YSYS.

Mendelson, 1996, pp. 280–285. This SUGI paper shows a couple of simple examples using Annotate.

CHAPTER 3

Simple Annotate Examples

3.1 Chapter Overview

Once created, the Annotate data–with its functions, coordinates, and associated variables–must be passed to a procedure capable of processing the information. Using either the ANNO= or the ANNOTATE= option in a SAS/GRAPH procedure such as GPLOT or GSLIDE causes the procedure to process the instructions contained in the Annotate data set.

Each of the following SAS/GRAPH procedure steps makes use of an Annotate data set named ORPHAN:

```
proc ganno annotate=orphan;
run;

proc gplot data=plotdata anno=orphan;
plot vvar*hvar;
run;

proc gplot data=plotdata;
plot vvar*hvar / annotate=orphan;
run;
```

When referencing the Annotate data set, you may use either the ANNOTATE= option or its abbreviation ANNO=.

More Information
A number of procedures, such as those in SAS/QC software and SAS/STAT software, also accept the use of Annotate data sets. Within SAS virtually all procedures that create high–resolution graphics can incorporate instructions stored in Annotate data sets. Specific examples shown with PROC SHEWART can be found in Claude, 1997.

3.2 WHAT - Adding Text

It is a very common desire to augment a plot with additional text. One of the features of the Annotate facility is the ability to place text anywhere on the graphics output area. The Annotate function LABEL is used to access this feature.

3.2.1 Adding text using PROC GANNO and PROC GSLIDE

The GANNO procedure is designed to display information contained in Annotate data sets. No other data or graphics information is shown. In addition to the Annotate information, PROC GSLIDE displays titles, notes, and footnotes.

In the following example, the absolute graphics output area percent coordinate system (XSYS & YSYS = '3') was specified for both X and Y. X=50 indicates a position 50 percent of the way across the graphics area as measured from the left side of the page. Y=50 indicates a position halfway up from the bottom of the graphics area.

A text string is placed at the center of the graphics display area. The Annotate data set is named SANDY, and it contains a single observation. The variables SIZE and STYLE are used to adjust the font and the size of the letters in the text string.

The following code was used to produce Figure 3.2.1a. Notice that although GOPTIONS BORDER ❶ is clearly specified, no border is produced. PROC GANNO ignores the TITLE ❷ definition and several of the graphics options, including BORDER.

```
filename filerefa "&pathcgm\wex3_2_1a.cgm";
filename filerefb "&pathcgm\wex3_2_1b.cgm";

goptions reset=all;
goptions device=cgmof971 gsfmode=replace;
*goptions device=win;

DATA SANDY ;
    LENGTH FUNCTION $8;
    RETAIN FUNCTION 'LABEL' XSYS YSYS '5' X Y 50;
    STYLE='brush';
    SIZE=8;
    TEXT='A Dog Called Sandy';
run;

goptions border; ❶

goptions gsfname=filerefa;
PROC GANNO ANNO=SANDY ;
title 'Placing Text Using GANNO'; ❷
footnote j=1 h=2 f=simplex 'Figure 3.2.1a';
RUN;
```

The data set SANDY contains the following observaion:

OBS	FUNCTION	XSYS	YSYS	X	Y	STYLE	SIZE	TEXT
1	LABEL	5	5	50	50	brush	8	A Dog Called Sandy

A Dog Called Sandy

Figure 3.2.1a *Simple label showing that titles, borders, and footnotes **are not** displayed when generated using PROC GANNO*

The same Annotate data set (SANDY) can be used with PROC GSLIDE to produce Figure 3.2.1b. This time the title, border, and footnote are displayed.

```
goptions gsfname=filerefb;
PROC gslide ANNO=SANDY ;
title 'Placing Text Using GSLIDE';
footnote j=1 h=2 f=simplex 'Figure 3.2.1b';
run;
quit;
```

Placing Text Using GSLIDE

A Dog Called Sandy

Figure 3.2.1b

Figure 3.2.1b *Simple label showing that titles, borders, and footnotes **are** displayed when generated using PROC GSLIDE*

3.2.2 Placing text on a scatter plot

Labels are often placed at a specific location on a scatter plot in order to be associated with particular points. In the following example a label (HIGH) is placed at a specific spot on a scatter plot. This requires that you know the coordinates of the point that is to have the label, which, in the following example, is X=4 and Y=2.5 ❶. The values of X and Y correspond to the X and Y axes (MONTH and DIAMONDS, respectively, in this example). To create this association, the values of XSYS and YSYS have been set to '2'.

In the data set ANNODAT.IMPORTS, imports of various precious items from three countries are recorded in millions of dollars. The plot following shows the imports of diamonds by Warbucks Industries from the country coded as SFO.

```
* Place a label on the value at month 4;
DATA ANNPLT;
    LENGTH FUNCTION $8 TEXT $5;
    RETAIN XSYS YSYS '2' STYLE 'SIMPLEX' ❷
      FUNCTION 'LABEL' ;
    SIZE = 2; ❸
    X=4;    Y=2.5; ❶
    TEXT='HIGH';
    OUTPUT;
RUN;

PROC GPLOT DATA=annodat.imports ANNO=ANNPLT;
    where co_code='SFO';
    PLOT diamonds * MONTH / vaxis=.5 to 2.5 by .5;
    SYMBOL1 L=1 V=NONE I=JOIN;
    TITLE1 H=2 F=SIMPLEX
          '1945 Diamond Imports in Millions';
    run;
    quit;
```

The coordinates X=4 and Y=2.5 ❶ determine the location of the label. The height of the characters and the font that is used are controlled through the use of the STYLE and SIZE variables. STYLE ❷ is a character variable that contains the name of the font that is to be used, and SIZE ❸, a numeric variable, designates the height of the text. In Figure 3.2, the font is set to SIMPLEX, and the size of the text is set to 2.

Note the use of the LENGTH statement to set the length of the FUNCTION and TEXT variables. Variables that receive a default length based on an assignment statement run the risk of truncation if a longer value is assigned later in the step. Using the LENGTH statement for variables such as FUNCTION, STYLE, and COLOR ensures that accidental truncation will not occur.

The Annotate data set, WORK.ANNPLT, contains the following observation:

OBS	FUNCTION	STYLE	TEXT	XSYS	YSYS	SIZE	X	Y
1	LABEL	SIMPLEX	HIGH	2	2	2	4	2.5

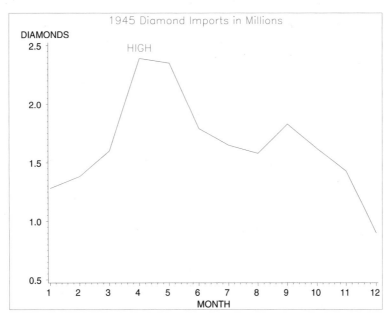

Figure 3.2.2 *Known data coordinate values can be used to place a label within the data area*

Unlike in this example, you may not know the location of the point of interest before the graph is drawn, so its placement will need to be data driven. The process of placing labels using values contained in the data is fairly easy to establish and is illustrated by Figures 4.4.1, 5.4.1a, 5.4.1b, 5.5.3a, 5.5.3b, and 5.6 in this monograph.

See Also

Section 4.4.1 shows a simple example that places labels on a graph using the data to determine the position.

More Information

A label is placed on a scatter plot by Gilbert, 1999.

3.3 WHAT - Drawing Lines Using Annotate

Annotate can be used to draw complete pictures, portions of diagrams, or lines that connect text to a point on the graph. The functions MOVE and DRAW are used to define this type of operation. MOVE is used to position the 'pen' on the display area using the coordinates X and Y. DRAW then creates a line by moving the pen to successive locations as specified in the observations that follow the MOVE.

In the next example, the XSYS and YSYS variables are set to '5' (absolute procedure output area percent). This means that values for X and Y will be interpreted as percentages of the graphics area relative to the lower left corner of the display area (excluding titles and footnotes). The following code produces Figure 3.3:

```
* Create the annotate data set DIAMOND;
DATA DIAMOND;
   LENGTH FUNCTION $8;
   * Use the percentages of the display area;
   * for coordinates;
   RETAIN XSYS YSYS '5' LINE 1;
   * Move the pen to the far left point;
   function='MOVE'; x=20; y=60; output;
   * Trace the outline of the diamond;
   function='DRAW'; x=50; y=30; output;
   function='DRAW'; x=80; y=60; output;
   function='DRAW'; x=70; y=70; output;
   function='DRAW'; x=30; y=70; output;
   function='DRAW'; x=20; y=60; output;
   function='DRAW'; x=80; y=60; output;
   * Move the pen to start drawing the facets;
   function='MOVE'; x=30; y=70; output;
   * Draw upper facets;
   function='DRAW'; x=40; y=60; output;
   function='DRAW'; x=50; y=70; output;
   function='DRAW'; x=60; y=60; output;
   function='DRAW'; x=70; y=70; output;
   * Draw lower facets;
   function='MOVE'; x=40; y=60; output;
   function='DRAW'; x=50; y=30; output;
   function='DRAW'; x=60; y=60; output;
run;

PROC GSLIDE ANNO=DIAMOND;
   TITLE1 H=2 F=SIMPLEX "Warbuck's Diamond";
   title2 H=1.5 f=simplex 'Using MOVE and DRAW';
   run;
   quit;
```

The RETAIN statement is used to define values for the three variables that are constants in this data set (XSYS, YSYS, and LINE). The first four observations of WORK.DIAMOND are as follows:

OBS	FUNCTION	XSYS	YSYS	LINE	X	Y
1	MOVE	5	5	1	20	60
2	DRAW	5	5	1	50	30
3	DRAW	5	5	1	80	60
4	DRAW	5	5	1	70	70

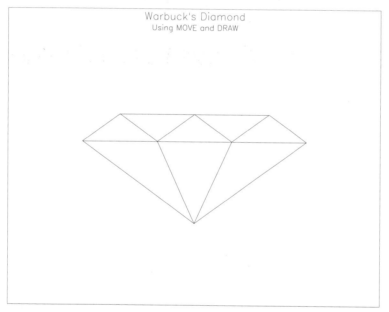

Figure 3.3 *A simple shape drawn by using a series of MOVEs and DRAWs*

Notice that the LENGTH statement was used to assign a length of $8 to FUNCTION. In some of the earlier releases of SAS/GRAPH (Release 6.04 and earlier) it was essential to specify this length. Although this is no longer the case, it is still generally considered a good idea to assign the length manually. When this is not done, and a variable's length is determined by its first use in an assignment statement, inadvertent truncation of values can occur. In the earlier example in this section, if the LENGTH statement had not been used, FUNCTION would have been given a length of $4 (by the statement FUNCTION='MOVE';). In this case it would not have been possible to later assign the value of LABEL to FUNCTION.

The MOVE and DRAW functions are not the only functions that can be used to draw lines and shapes. The POLY and POLYCONT functions are designed to create polygons. The PIE function can be used to create circles and circular sectors, and the BAR function to create rectangles. These have an advantage over the MOVE and DRAW functions because they automatically connect the last point to the first point, thereby completing the shape.

More Information

Chinn, 1997, contains examples that use MOVE and DRAW.

CHAPTER 4

Building the Annotate Data Set

4.1   Chapter Overview

The Annotate data set is created using many of the same tools that are used to create other SAS data sets. Remember that an Annotate data set is just an ordinary SAS data set. What is special about an Annotate data set is that the Annotate facility can make use of only specific variable names, and these often have prescribed attributes. This chapter discusses several aspects of creating this specialized data set.

The Annotate data set can be built

- by using assignment statements

- based on information contained in a flat file

- from an existing SAS data set

- by using Annotate macros (see Chapter 6).

4.2   Using Assignment Statements

The Annotate data set can be built from scratch by using assignment statements. This technique is best employed when only a few observations are needed. The example below creates an Annotate data set that is passed to PROC GSLIDE. The data set has only three observations and nine variables, and each observation is used to create a single text string on the graph. Four of these variables (FUNCTION, XSYS, YSYS, and X) have constant values that are assigned with the RETAIN statement ❶. The values of the remainder of the variables vary for one or more observations and receive their values through assignment statements.

```
* USE PROC GSLIDE AND Annotate TO CREATE;
* A CLASSIFIED AD FOR ANNIE.;
DATA ANNIE;
LENGTH FUNCTION COLOR STYLE $8;
RETAIN FUNCTION 'LABEL' XSYS YSYS '5' X 50; ❶
     COLOR='BLUE';
     STYLE='SCRIPT';
     SIZE=4;
```

```
        TEXT='Home Wanted                ❷
        Y=75;
        OUTPUT;

        STYLE='DUPLEX';
        SIZE=2;
        TEXT='GIRL - WITHOUT EYES';
        Y=50;
        OUTPUT;

        COLOR='GREEN';
        STYLE='TRIPLEX';
        TEXT='Has Dog / Will Travel';
        Y=30;
        OUTPUT;
    run;

    PROC GSLIDE ANNO=ANNIE;
        TITLE1 F=SWISS H=3 'Classified Ad';
        run;
```

Because the RETAIN statement is non-executable, it is more efficient than an assignment statement when defining variables with constant values. To avoid truncation and to make sure that variables have compatible attributes when Annotate data sets are combined, it is a good idea to specify the length of character variables. Either the LENGTH or the RETAIN statement can be used. In the above example, the length of the variable TEXT is determined in an assignment statement ❷. It would have been more appropriate to use a LENGTH statement, which would avoid the need to use the trailing blanks.

In this example the horizontal position (X) is constant ❶ while the vertical position (Y) varies for each observation. Because the XSYS and YSYS variables are set to '5' (absolute procedure output area percent), the X and Y variable values are percentages. The font is specified by STYLE and the size of the text is controlled through SIZE.

The Annotate data set ANNIE contains the following records:

OBS	FUNCTION	COLOR	STYLE	XSYS	YSYS	X	SIZE	TEXT	Y
1	LABEL	BLUE	SCRIPT	5	5	50	4	Home Wanted	75
2	LABEL	BLUE	DUPLEX	5	5	50	2	GIRL-WITHOUT EYES	50
3	LABEL	GREEN	TRIPLEX	5	5	50	2	Has Dog / Will Travel	30

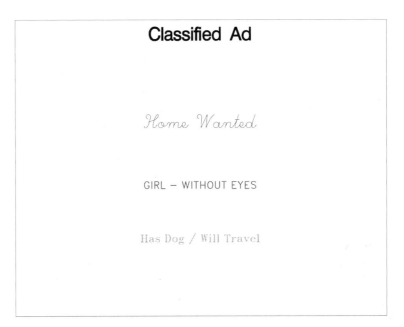

Figure 4.2 *The Annotate observations used to create this ad were created using assignment statements*

See Also

The example in Section 3.3 also builds the Annotate data set using a series of assignment statements.

4.3 Reading a Flat Control File

In Section 4.2, the data set ANNIE was created by using assignment statements. However, this becomes cumbersome if the number of Annotate observations is large. An alternate way to build the Annotate data set is to base it on a raw or flat file that can be read into a SAS data set by using the INPUT statement. The raw data file should contain all necessary information required by Annotate.

The following example draws a picture through a series of MOVEs and DRAWs. The value of FUNCTION and the coordinates are read into the Annotate data set (DIAMOND) by using the INPUT statement. Three variables (XSYS, YSYS, and LINE) have constant values that are assigned in the RETAIN statement.

```
* USE THE DATALINES STATEMENT TO PRESENT THE DATA;
DATA DIAMOND;
     LENGTH FUNCTION $8;
     RETAIN XSYS YSYS '5' LINE 1;
     INPUT FUNCTION X Y;
     X = X*10 + 20;
     Y = Y*10 + 30;
     DATALINES;
     MOVE 0 3
     DRAW 3 0
     DRAW 6 3
     DRAW 5 4
     DRAW 1 4
     DRAW 0 3
     DRAW 6 3
     MOVE 1 4
     DRAW 2 3
     DRAW 3 4
     DRAW 4 3
     DRAW 5 4
     MOVE 2 3
     DRAW 3 0
     DRAW 4 3
     ;

PROC GSLIDE ANNO=DIAMOND;
     TITLE1 H=2 "Daddy Warbuck's Diamond";
     run;
     quit;
```

The size and position of the diamond can be changed by adjusting the values of X and Y. In this example the variables XSYS and YSYS are set to '5'. Consequently, the values of X and Y are interpreted as percentages of the screen. The values in the data are multiplied by 10 to increase the size of the drawing, which is then shifted (centered) by adding 20 horizontal and 30 vertical units.

The first four observations of the DIAMOND data set contain the following data:

OBS	FUNCTION	XSYS	YSYS	LINE	X	Y
1	MOVE	5	5	1	20	60
2	DRAW	5	5	1	50	30
3	DRAW	5	5	1	80	60
4	DRAW	5	5	1	70	70

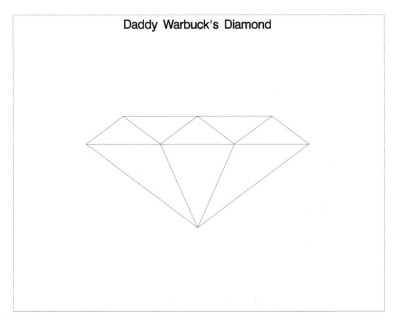

Figure 4.3 *The series of Annotate statements were built from a flat control file*

See Also

The same graph is created in Section 3.3 by using a series of assignment statements.

4.4 Building upon an Existing SAS Data Set

When the graphics display depends on an established SAS data set, that data set can often be used to build the Annotate data set as well. This technique is especially useful when you need to place labels or text strings at a location that is to be determined by the data itself.

4.4.1 Adding Annotate variables to the plot data

The data set to be plotted and the Annotate data set do not necessarily need to be distinct. Annotate ignores any variables that are not in the Annotate dictionary. More specifically, Annotate looks only for the specific variables that are used by the FUNCTION defined in the current observation.

This example adds a label to each point that has a Y value (diamond imports in millions of dollars) greater than 2. Two items of information are taken from the data that will be used by Annotate; that is, the value of the data point and the location that the point will be plotted on the graph.

```
* label all months with imports exceeding $2 million;
data imports;
   set annodat.imports;
   length function $8 text $5;
❶ retain xsys ysys '2'  ❸ style 'simplex'
         function 'label' position '3'  ❹ size 1.5;
   where co_code='SFO';
   if diamonds ge 2 then do;  ❷
      x=month;
      y=diamonds;
      text=put(diamonds,5.2);
   end;
run;
```

```
* Annotate and GPLOT use the same data set;
proc gplot data=imports anno=imports;   ❺
   plot diamonds * month;
   symbol1 l=1 v=dot i=join;
   title1 h=2 'Diamond Imports From SFO in 1945';
run;
quit;
```

Although the Annotate variables defined in the RETAIN statement ❶ are present in all observations, the location variables X and Y have missing values for all observations except those that meet the specified criteria ❷. Thus, there are only two annotated labels.

The Annotate variables XSYS and YSYS are set to '2', causing the values of Y and X to use the same axes as the two plot variables DIAMONDS and MONTH ❸. Because FUNCTION is set to 'LABEL', Y and X will place TEXT (containing the value of the variable DIAMONDS) on the graph next to the appropriate data point.

The variable POSITION ❹ determines where the text string is to be placed relative to the (X,Y) location. POSITION='3' indicates that the text will start immediately to the right and above the plotted symbol. This variable is discussed further in Section 5.3.1.

Because WORK.IMPORTS contains both the plot information and the information controlling the annotation process, the data set is mentioned twice in the GPLOT statement ❺. Values of selected variables from the first six observations of WORK.IMPORTS are shown next. Notice that although Annotate variables created with the RETAIN statement are never missing, only observations with non-missing values of TEXT, X, and Y are used by Annotate.

OBS	DIAMONDS	MONTH	FUNCTION	TEXT	XSYS	YSYS	STYLE	POSITION	SIZE	X	Y
1	1.28	1	label		2	2	simplex	3	1.5	.	.
2	1.38	2	label		2	2	simplex	3	1.5	.	.
3	1.60	3	label		2	2	simplex	3	1.5	.	.
4	2.39	4	label	2.39	2	2	simplex	3	1.5	4	2.39
5	2.35	5	label	2.35	2	2	simplex	3	1.5	5	2.35
6	1.79	6	label		2	2	simplex	3	1.5	.	.

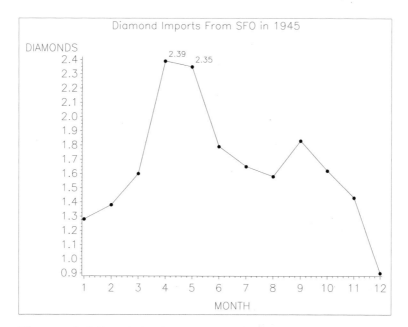

Figure 4.4.1 *Label placement can be determined directly from the data*

4.4.2 Creating a separate Annotate data set

The example in Section 4.4.1 adds the Annotate variables to the same data set that is to be plotted. Although this works quite well and produces the desired result, it is an inefficient approach. Only two of the observations in IMPORTS are actually used to produce annotation; however, all the observations contain Annotate variables.

The following example produces the same result as shown in Figure 4.4.1. Rather than create a single data set, the DATA step separates the incoming data into two data sets (the data to be plotted and the Annotate data set). The Annotate data set (DIANNO) contains only the Annotate variables ❶ and two observations ❷. The data set IMPORTS contains only those variables needed to generate the plot ❸ and those observations with the country code (CO_CODE) of 'SFO' ❹. The two data sets are then called separately in the GPLOT statement ❺ by using the DATA= and ANNO= options.

```
* label all months with imports exceeding $2 million;
data imports(keep=diamonds month) ❸
     dianno (keep=xsys ysys style function position
                  size x y text) ❶ ;
   set annodat.imports(keep=co_code diamonds month);
   length function $8 text $5;
   retain xsys ysys '2' style 'simplex'
          function 'label' position '3' size 1.5;
   where co_code='SFO';
   output imports; ❹
   if diamonds ge 2 then do;
      * Conditional observation for Annotate;
      x=month;
      y=diamonds;
      text=put(diamonds,5.2);
      output dianno; ❷
   end;
run;


* Annotate and GPLOT use separate data sets;
proc gplot data=imports anno=dianno; ❺
   plot diamonds * month;
   symbol1 l=1 v=dot i=join;
   title1 h=2 'Diamond Imports From SFO in 1945';
run;
quit;
```

More Information

Additional examples of the use of Annotate labels can be found in several sources: Dorr, 1998; Kenny, 1998; and Vierkant, 1998.

CHAPTER 5

Enhancing Output from
SAS/GRAPH® Procedures

5.1 Chapter Overview

One of the primary purposes of Annotate is to augment the graphs and charts produced by various SAS/GRAPH procedures. Sections 4.4.1 and 4.4.2 added simple labels to graphs generated by PROC GPLOT.

As was discussed in detail in earlier sections, the Annotate data set must contain information about both the appearance of the text (**how**) and the location (**where**) that the text is to be placed on the graph.

The text's attributes are controlled by assigning values to specific Annotate variables. Section 5.2 introduces some of these variables, and Section 5.3 discusses how to control text location.

More Information
Although not demonstrated by example in this monograph, it is possible also to use annotation on three-dimensional graphs (Pratter, 1997, and Carpenter, 1988).

5.2 Controlling Text Appearance

Usually, when you are placing text on a graphic, the selected function will be LABEL. Annotate gives you a great deal of control over text appearance and placement through the use of attribute variables, some of which are detailed in Table 5.2. Most of the text control options that are available in the TITLE and SYMBOL statements are also available in Annotate. The primary difference, of course, is that you specify variables rather than options to achieve this control.

TITLE/SYMBOL OPTION	Annotate Variable	PURPOSE
Font=	STYLE	Designates the graphic font.
Height=	SIZE	Determines the character size.
Rotate=	ROTATE	Rotates individual characters.
Angle=	ANGLE	Changes the angle of the text line.
Color=	COLOR	Assigns the color for the text.

Table 5.2 *Many of the text appearance options available in TITLE and FOOTNOTE statements are also available as Annotate attribute variables*

In TITLE and SYMBOL statements the font is specified by using the FONT= option. However, in Annotate data sets, the variable STYLE is used to designate the font. Because STYLE can take on the value of the name of any font that is available to the graphics device, it is wise to give this variable a length of $8 to avoid truncation issues. Usually STYLE takes on the font names that are shown in Chapter 6 of *SAS/GRAPH Software: Reference, Version 6, First Edition*, (pp.168–174).

The size of the text is controlled by the SIZE variable. This numeric variable is used similarly to the HEIGHT= (H=) option in the TITLE and SYMBOL statements.

Normally the text is added along a horizontal baseline. However the ANGLE variable can be used to specify the number of degrees (0 to 360) to pivot the entire line. The angle is measured counterclockwise from the horizontal baseline.

It is also possible to rotate the individual characters within a text string. The ROTATE variable specifies the angle of rotation for each individual character. Very often the ROTATE and ANGLE options are used together on the same text string.

5.3 Text Location

The physical location (**where**) of the text is determined by the values of the variables X and Y and the graphics system variables XSYS and YSYS. Refinements to the location can be made by using additional variables such as POSITION.

More Information

Griffin, 1998, gives several examples of creating subscripts and superscripts.

5.3.1 Relationship between POSITION and FUNCTION='LABEL'

The POSITION variable places the text relative to the point established by X and Y. This variable assumes one of 15 values and allows you to make sure that the label itself does not interfere with other points on the plot.

POSITION takes on the values from '1' to '9' and 'A' to 'F.' In the following example 15 points are plotted, each with a label of POS=x, where the x is the value of POSITION.

```
* DEMONSTRATE THE POSITION VARIABLE WITH
* FUNCTION=LABEL;
DATA PLTDAT;
     LENGTH POS $1;
     INPUT POS $ X Y;
     CARDS;
     1   1   1
     2   2   2
     3   3   3
     4   4   4
     5   5   5
     6   6   6
     7   7   7
     8   8   8
     9   9   9
     A   10  10
     B   11  11
     C   12  12
```

```
        D   13 13
        E   14 14
        F   15 15
        RUN;

DATA ANNDAT;
        SET PLTDAT;
        LENGTH FUNCTION $8 TEXT $15;
        RETAIN STYLE 'SIMPLEX' XSYS YSYS '2'
            FUNCTION 'LABEL' SIZE 1.5;
        TEXT = 'POS=' || POS;
        POSITION = POS;
        RUN;

PROC GPLOT DATA=PLTDAT ANNO=ANNDAT;
        PLOT Y * X;
        SYMBOL1 v=dot c=black;
        TITLE1 H=2 F=SIMPLEX 'LABEL POSITIONS';
        run;
        quit;
```

The Annotate data set ANNDAT contains the following observations:

OBS	POS	X	Y	FUNCTION	TEXT	STYLE	XSYS	YSYS	SIZE	POSITION
1	1	1	1	LABEL	POS=1	SIMPLEX	2	2	1.5	1
2	2	2	2	LABEL	POS=2	SIMPLEX	2	2	1.5	2
3	3	3	3	LABEL	POS=3	SIMPLEX	2	2	1.5	3
4	4	4	4	LABEL	POS=4	SIMPLEX	2	2	1.5	4
5	5	5	5	LABEL	POS=5	SIMPLEX	2	2	1.5	5
6	6	6	6	LABEL	POS=6	SIMPLEX	2	2	1.5	6
7	7	7	7	LABEL	POS=7	SIMPLEX	2	2	1.5	7
8	8	8	8	LABEL	POS=8	SIMPLEX	2	2	1.5	8
9	9	9	9	LABEL	POS=9	SIMPLEX	2	2	1.5	9
10	A	10	10	LABEL	POS=A	SIMPLEX	2	2	1.5	A
11	B	11	11	LABEL	POS=A	SIMPLEX	2	2	1.5	B
12	C	12	12	LABEL	POS=C	SIMPLEX	2	2	1.5	C
13	D	13	13	LABEL	POS=D	SIMPLEX	2	2	1.5	D
14	E	14	14	LABEL	POS=E	SIMPLEX	2	2	1.5	E
15	F	15	15	LABEL	POS=F	SIMPLEX	2	2	1.5	F

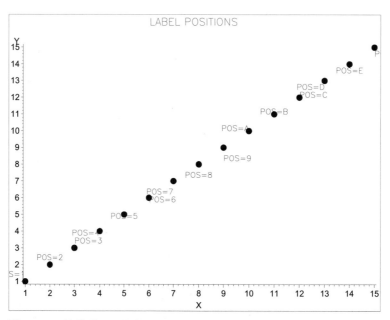

Figure 5.3.1 Label placement around a specified location is handled through the use of the POSITION variable

In this graph the location of each label depends on the value of the variable POSITION. Notice that Annotate does not protect you when you place the labels. The label for POSITION='1' is written outside the DATA area and covers a portion of the axis information. Similarly, the label for POSITION='F' falls almost completely out of the graphic output area and is truncated. You may have noticed also that several of the labels fall on or overlap with the plotted symbol, such as POSITION='4', '6', 'A', and 'C'. Sometimes this overlap can be prevented by storing one or more blank characters as part of the label, by changing the symbol or label size, or by selecting a different value for POSITION.

More Information

SAS/GRAPH Software: Reference, Version 6, First Edition, pp. 521–524, gives a detailed description of the placement of the labels for each of the values of POSITION.

Version 7 and 8 users should consult *SAS OnlineDoc.*

Griffin, 1995, pp. 1067–1069. The use of POSITION is described using a series of graphs.

5.4 Enhancing Scatter Plots

Because of the various levels of control within Annotate, it is possible to create all types of annotation on scatter plots, such as the ones created by GPLOT. One of the most typical applications was demonstrated in Sections 4.4.1 and 4.4.2, where a label was attached to a specific location on a plot.

5.4.1 Adding labels to points

The examples in Sections 4.4.1 and 4.4.2 add labels to points that have a Y value that exceeds 2 (imports of diamonds in millions of dollars). The attributes of the labels can be changed by adding variables to the Annotate data set (DIANNO).

```
* label all months with imports exceeding $2 million;
data imports(keep=diamonds month)
     dianno (keep=xsys ysys style function position
                  size angle rotate x y text);
   set annodat.imports(keep=co_code diamonds month);
   length function $8 text $5;
   retain xsys ysys '2'
             ❶style 'simplex'  ❷size 2
             ❸angle 20  ❹rotate -20
             function 'label'  ❺position '3';
   where co_code='SFO';
   output imports;
   if diamonds ge 2 then do;
      * Conditional observation for Annotate;
      x=month;
      y=diamonds;
      text=put(diamonds,5.2);
      output dianno;
   end;
run;
```

In this example the following text attributes are specified:

❶ STYLE   sets font to SIMPLEX.

❷ SIZE   specifies that character height is 2 units.

❸ ANGLE   raises the entire label at an angle of 20 degrees.

❹ ROTATE   rotates each individual letter within the label back (minus degrees) to the horizontal.

❺ POSITION   places the text above and to the right of the plotted point.

The selected data for country code SFO is shown below and plotted in Figure 5.4.1a.

OBS	DIAMONDS	GOLD	SILVER	DATE	CO_CODE	MONTH
25	1.28	2.44	4.34	15JAN45	SFO	1
26	1.38	2.58	4.60	15FEB45	SFO	2
27	1.60	2.05	1.56	15MAR45	SFO	3
28	2.39	1.76	1.93	15APR45	SFO	4
29	2.35	1.58	1.82	15MAY45	SFO	5
30	1.79	1.60	1.20	15JUN45	SFO	6
31	1.65	1.85	4.25	15JUL45	SFO	7
32	1.58	1.64	1.84	15AUG45	SFO	8
33	1.83	2.01	3.08	15SEP45	SFO	9
34	1.62	2.14	1.81	15OCT45	SFO	10
35	1.43	2.02	1.33	15NOV45	SFO	11
36	0.90	2.21	8.23	15DEC45	SFO	12

The Annotate data set WORK.DIANNO contains the following observations:

OBS	FUNCTION	TEXT	XSYS	YSYS	STYLE	SIZE	ANGLE	ROTATE	POSITION	X	Y
1	label	2.39	2	2	simplex	2	20	−20	3	4	2.39
2	label	2.35	2	2	simplex	2	20	−20	3	5	2.35

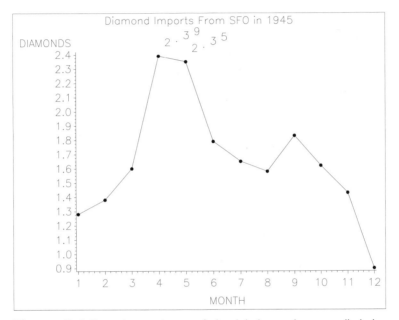

Figure 5.4.1a *The attributes of the label can be controlled through a series of Annotate variables, such as, STYLE, ANGLE, SIZE, and ROTATE*

Sometimes it is not convenient to place the text next to the point. Often a line can be drawn from the point to another location on the graph. This becomes a multiple-step process, but it is not necessarily more complex.

In the following example we are going to place a single label (for the month with the largest dollar value of imported diamonds), but we will place it on the far right side of the graphic area.

```
* Determine the month with the maximum # of imports;
proc summary data=annodat.imports
                      (where=( co_code='SFO'));
   var diamonds;
   output out=stats max=y ❶
                      maxid(diamonds(month))=x;
   run;

* Create the label using Annotate;
data dianno (keep=xsys ysys style function size line
                  x y text position);
   set stats; ❷
   length function $8 text $5;
   retain xsys ysys '2' line 33
          style 'simplex' position 'c';
   * Specify the start point for the line;
   function = 'move'; output; ❸
   * Draw to edge of plot;
   function = 'draw'; ❹
      size=2; x=11;   output;
   * Add the label;
   function='label';
   text=put(y,5.2); ❺
   output;
run;

* Annotate and GPLOT use separate data sets;
proc gplot data=annodat.imports
                 (where=(co_code='SFO'))
                 anno=dianno;
   plot diamonds * month;
   symbol1 l=1 v=dot i=join;
   title1 h=2 'Diamond Imports From SFO in 1945';
run;
quit;
```

❶ Use PROC SUMMARY to create a data set containing the maximum imports and the month of the maximum. Note that the statistics are saved in the variables X and Y, which will be used directly by Annotate.

❷ The STATS data set from the PROC SUMMARY step is used to create the Annotate data set.

❸ Move to the maximum point. The values for X and Y come directly from STATS.

❹ Draw to the side of the graph. Y remains constant and X changes.

❺ Create a LABEL at the end of the dotted line.

The Annotate data set WORK.DIANNO contains the following observations:

OBS	Y	X	FUNCTION	TEXT	XSYS	YSYS	LINE	STYLE	POSITION	SIZE
1	2.39	4	move		2	2	33	simplex	c	.
2	2.39	11	draw		2	2	33	simplex	c	2
3	2.39	11	label	2.39	2	2	33	simplex	c	2

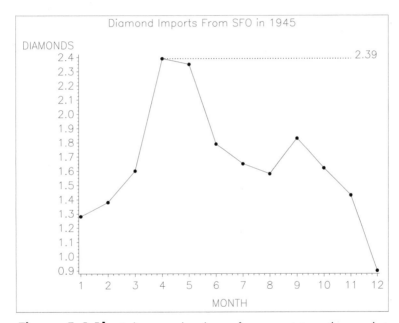

Figure 5.4.1b *A line can be drawn from a point on the graph to an offset label*

More Information

Kirk, 1998, uses lines to add legends, boxes, and labels.

5.4.2 Using Annotate to label an axis

Often when you want to place annotated labels on one of the axes, you need to use a combination of different XSYS and YSYS values. In the following example, a special label is placed under the spring months (3 through 6 - Daddy Warbucks defines spring his own way). The horizontal placement is made using the actual horizontal axis scale (XSYS = '2'); however, the vertical value is placed as a percentage in the absolute procedure output area (YSYS = '5'). The code produces Figure 5.4.2.

```
* Create the label using Annotate;
data spring (keep=xsys ysys style function size line
                x y text position);
   length function style $8 text $6; ❻
   retain xsys '2' ysys '5' line 1
          position 'E';

   * Draw the arrows;
   * Locate the left side;
   function = 'symbol'; ❶
   x=3; y= 6;
   size=2;
   style = 'marker';
   text='G';
   output;
   * Locate the right side;
   x = 6;
   output;

   * Prep to do the line;
   function = 'move'; ❷
   x=3; y=4.5;
   output;

   * Draw the line;
   function = 'draw'; ❸
   x=6;   size=3; ❹
   output;

   * Insert a label;
   function = 'label'; ❺
   x=4.5; y= 5;
   size=2;
   style = 'brush'; ❻
   text='Spring';
   output;
run;
```

```
* Annotate and GPLOT use separate data sets;
proc gplot data=annodat.imports (where=(co_code='SFO'))
               anno=spring;
   plot diamonds * month;
   symbol1 l=1 v=dot i=join;
   title1 h=2 'Diamond Imports From SFO in 1945';
   label month = '    Month'; ❼
run;
quit;
```

❶ The FUNCTION='SYMBOL' places a symbol at the specified location. In this case the Y value (Y=6) is a percentage from the bottom of the procedure output area, while the X value (X=3) corresponds to month 3.

❷ Move to the start of the underline.

❸ Draw the line to the right endpoint.

❹ When the FUNCTION is 'DRAW', the variable SIZE specifies the thickness of the line.

❺ Setting FUNCTION='LABEL' places the word 'Spring' under the line.

❻ STYLE has been added to the LENGTH statement. It is a good idea to include all character Annotate variables that take on varying lengths in the LENGTH statement. This prevents a very common problem of value truncation.

❼ Extra spaces are added to the label for the horizontal axis so that it shifts to the right to avoid any conflict with the annotated 'Spring.'

The Annotate data set WORK.SPRING contains the following observations:

OBS	FUNCTION	TEXT	XSYS	YSYS	LINE	POSITION	X	Y	SIZE	STYLE
1	symbol	G	2	5	1	E	3.0	6.0	2	marker
2	symbol	G	2	5	1	E	6.0	6.0	2	marker
3	move	G	2	5	1	E	3.0	4.5	2	marker
4	draw	G	2	5	1	E	6.0	4.5	3	marker
5	label	Spring	2	5	1	E	4.5	5.9	2	brush

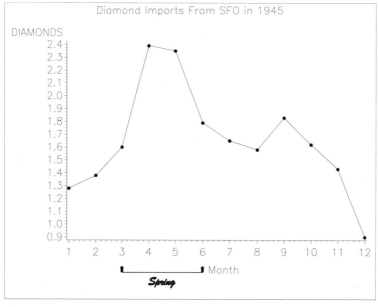

Figure 5.4.2 *Labels outside of the Data Area can still be tied to the horizontal or vertical axis*

More Information

A similar, but more complex, example of drawing under an axis can be found in Kenny, 1998.

5.4.3 Adding a second horizontal axis

In this example a second horizontal axis has been drawn at the top of the data area. Three different values of XSYS and YSYS are used to place the line.

1   Absolute data area using percentages

2   Absolute data area using the axis values

7   Relative data area using percentages.

Each of these coordinate systems applies just to the data area or the portion of the graph that is defined by the two axes. The axis value coordinate systems (2 and 8) use the actual axis values when defining the location associated with the values of X and Y. Percentages (1 and 7) allow us to specify a location on the axis without knowing the exact value of the axis.

Usually you want to specify a location based on a specific set of coordinates that are measured from the lower left corner of the coordinate system (absolute). However, sometimes you need to use an offset value. The relative coordinate systems (7 and 8) create an offset value from the coordinate defined in the previous observation in the Annotate data set. When YSYS='7' and Y=4, the current action occurs 4 percentage units above the last Y coordinate. Sometimes, as in the example shown next, the result will be outside the data area, even though YSYS is set to the data area coordinate system.

❶The line is drawn with MOVE and DRAW, and its endpoints are located by using XSYS and YSYS values of '1'. This is an absolute percentage coordinate system, and it allows us to locate the extreme top left ❷ (Y=100 and X=0) and the top right ❸(Y=100 and X=100) corners of the plot area.

Tick marks are placed as symbols, which are located with XSYS = '2' ❹. The tick mark values are placed above the tick marks by offsetting them with a relative percentage ❺(YSYS='7') of 4%.

```
* Create the axis using Annotate;
data spring (keep=xsys ysys style function size line
                 x y text position);
   length function $8 text $6;
   retain ysys '5' line 1 size 2
          position 'E';

   * Prep to do the line;
   function = 'move';
   xsys = '1'; ysys= '1';  ❶
   x=0; y=100;  ❷
   output;

   * Draw the line;
   function = 'draw';
   x=100;  ❸
   output;

* Add tick marks;
   xsys='2';
   style = 'simplex';
```

```
      do x = 1 to 12;
         xsys = '2'; ysys='1';
         y=100;
         function='symbol';
         text = '|'; ❹
         output;
         ysys = '7'; ❺
         y = 4; ❻
         text = left(put(x,2.));
         output;
      end;
   run;

   * Annotate and GPLOT use separate data sets;
   proc gplot data=annodat.imports
                   (where=(co_code='SFO'))anno=spring;
      plot diamonds * month;
      symbol1 l=1 v=dot i=join;
      title1 h=2 'Diamond Imports From SFO in 1945';
      label month = 'Month';
   run;
   quit;
```

The first ten observations of the Annotate data set WORK.SPRING appear here. The first two observations draw the axis, and the remaining observations alternately supply the vertical tick mark and the number. The code produces Figure 5.4.3.

OBS	FUNCTION	TEXT	YSYS	LINE	SIZE	POSITION	XSYS	X	Y	STYLE
1	move		1	1	2	E	1	0	100	
2	draw		1	1	2	E	1	100	100	
3	symbol	|	1	1	2	E	2		100	simplex
4	symbol	1	7	1	2	E	2		4	simplex
5	symbol	|	1	1	2	E	2	2	100	simplex
6	symbol	2	7	1	2	E	2	2	4	simplex
7	symbol	|	1	1	2	E	2	3	100	simplex
8	symbol	3	7	1	2	E	2		4	simplex
9	symbol	|	1	1	2	E	2	4	100	simplex
10	symbol	4	7	1	2	E	2	4	4	simplex

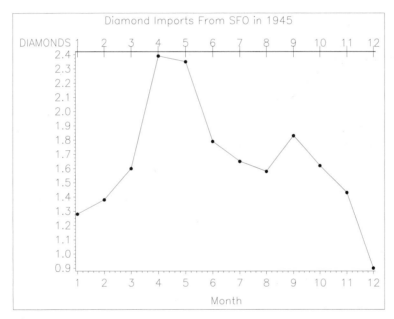

Figure 5.4.3 *A second horizontal axis has been added at the top of the graph*

As a matter of preference, other symbols could have been selected for the tick marks on the second horizontal axis.

5.5 Enhancing GCHART Histograms

When Annotate is used to modify graphs created by PROC GCHART, we need to look at the graph differently from when it is created by PROC GPLOT. Plots created by PROC GPLOT always have an X and Y axis and use both the X and Y variables to determine the location for an annotate action. This is not necessarily true for graphs created by PROC GCHART because they do not have the same axis structure as plots created by PROC GPLOT. Often this means that special Annotate variables are required to handle the placement of symbols and labels.

5.5.1 Special GCHART Annotate variables

Some charts, such as histograms (known as bar charts in recent SAS documentation), seem to have both vertical and horizontal axes, while pie charts seem to have neither. Instead, these charts have MIDPOINT, GROUP, and RESPONSE axes. Annotate labels and symbols require orientation to these axes.

This association between the chart's axes and Annotate is accomplished through the use of special Annotate variables that are used only with PROC GCHART. These variables are as follows:

MIDPOINT   identifies the variable used to establish the midpoint axis.

GROUP   identifies a grouping variable when present.

X or Y   associates the response axis value.

On a vertical histogram the variable Y designates the vertical (response) axis, while on a horizontal histogram, the variable Y is not used and the horizontal axis variable X designates the response axis. In both cases the MIDPOINT or GROUP variables designate the location on the axis other than the response axis. For a vertical histogram, for instance, the two variables MIDPOINT and Y would form the coordinate pair. This is illustrated in the following sections.

5.5.2 Histograms with error bars

The vertical histogram (Figure 5.5.2) produced by the following code shows the average monthly dollar amount of diamonds (in millions of $) imported by Daddy Warbucks from the three coded countries. Error bars (two standard deviations) have been added.

```
* Determine the average imports for each country;
proc summary data=annodat.imports;
   by co_code;
   var diamonds;
   output out=mean mean=average std=std n=n;
   run;

* Create the axis using Annotate;
data bars (keep=xsys ysys function size line
               midpoint y when);
   set mean;
   length function $8;
   retain xsys ysys '2' when 'a' ❶
          line 1 size 3;

   * Prep to do the line;
   function = 'move'; ❷
   midpoint=co_code; y=average; ❸
   output;

   * Draw the line below the bar;
   function = 'draw'; ❹
   y=average - 2*std;
   output;

   * Draw the line above the bar;
   function = 'draw'; ❺
   y=average + 2*std;
   output;
run;

axis1 order = (0 to 6 by 1)
      label = (a=90 '$ in Millions');

* Annotate and GPLOT use separate data sets;
proc gchart data=mean
            anno=bars;
   vbar co_code / sumvar=average type=mean
                  raxis = axis1; ❻
   title1 h=2 'Average Diamond Imports in 1945';
run;
quit;
```

❶ The WHEN variable determines if the annotation occurs before (WHEN='b' – the default) or after (WHEN='a') the rest of the graph is produced. In this example the lower part of the annotated line would not be visible with WHEN='b.' The value of WHEN can be in either upper- or lowercase.

❷ Move to the top center of the bar, which has the coordinates shown in ❸.

❸ The variable MIDPOINT identifies the horizontal location. X is **not** used. The same variable (CO_CODE) is used both in the Annotate data set to fix the value of MIDPOINT and in the VBAR statement as the midpoint variable.

❹ Draw the line to a minus two standard deviations.

❺ Draw the line to two standard deviations above the top of the bar.

❻ The vertical axis is the response axis, and it is tied to an AXIS statement by using the RAXIS= option.

The data set BARS is used to annotate the error bars. Each vertical bar is created by a MOVE and two DRAWs. Notice that the horizontal position of each bar is fixed by using the MIDPOINT variable, which also contains the country code (CO_CODE).

OBS	FUNCTION	XSYS	YSYS	WHEN	LINE	SIZE	MIDPOINT	Y
1	move	2	2	a	1	3	AZU	3.34417
2	draw	2	2	a	1	3	AZU	1.23970
3	draw	2	2	a	1	3	AZU	5.44863
4	move	2	2	a	1	3	LIV	1.97333
5	draw	2	2	a	1	3	LIV	0.42886
6	draw	2	2	a	1	3	LIV	3.51781
7	move	2	2	a	1	3	SFO	1.65000
8	draw	2	2	a	1	3	SFO	0.81473
9	draw	2	2	a	1	3	SFO	2.48527

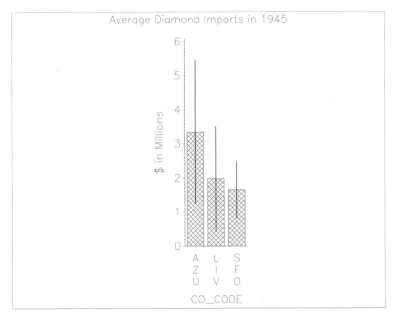

Figure 5.5.2 *Vertical error bars, based on the plotted values, are added using a series of MOVEs and DRAWs*

5.5.3 Histogram labels

It is quite common for you to need to place labels over the top of, or next to, the histogram bars. The principles are the same as shown in the previous example. Primarily, the vertical and horizontal location of the label must be determined, and the Annotate variables used will depend on the type of chart being produced.

Placing text above histogram bars

As in the previous example, the MIDPOINT variable is used instead of the X or Y variable for vertical or horizontal histograms respectively. The following example adds a label to the top of each vertical bar and produces Figure 5.5.3a.

```
proc sort data=annodat.imports
          out=imports;
   by month;
   run;

* Determine the average imports for each month;
proc summary data=imports;
   by month;
   var diamonds;
   output out=mean mean=mean;
   run;

* Create the axis  using Annotate;
data anno (keep=xsys ysys function size text angle
               style position
               midpoint y); ❶
   set mean;
   length function $8;
   retain xsys ysys '2'  position '3' angle 55
          function 'label'
          size 2 style 'simplex';

   rename month=midpoint; ❶
   y = mean;
   text = left(put(mean,5.2));
run;

axis1 order = (0 to 4 by 1)
      label = (a=90 '$ in Millions');
axis2 label = ('Month');

pattern1 color=red value=empty;

proc gchart data=mean;
   vbar month  ❷/ type=mean sumvar=mean
                  anno=anno discrete
                  raxis=axis1 maxis=axis2; ❸
   TITLE1 'Average Diamond Imports for 1945';
   run;
   quit;
```

❶   MIDPOINT is used instead of X to place the label horizontally.

❷   Because MONTH is the midpoint variable in the VBAR statement, it provides the value of the Annotate variable MIDPOINT.

❸   The MAXIS (midpoint axis) option points to the AXIS2 statement that controls the label for the horizontal axis.

The first four observations of the data set ANNO include the following:

OBS	MIDPOINT	FUNCTION	XSYS	YSYS	POSITION	ANGLE	SIZE	STYLE	Y	TEXT
1	1	label	2	2	3	55	2	simplex	1.21333	1.21
2	2	label	2	2	3	55	2	simplex	1.68000	1.68
3	3	label	2	2	3	55	2	simplex	2.27667	2.28
4	4	label	2	2	3	55	2	simplex	2.92000	2.92

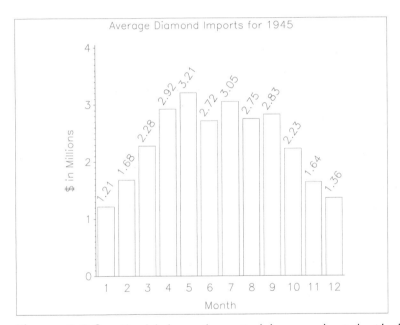

Figure 5.5.3a *The labels on the vertical bars are located with the Annotate variable MIDPOINT*

More Information

Several good examples of histograms with labels and error bars can be found in Elkin, 1997.

Placing text inside histogram bars

Because you can control the location of the label by setting the value of the variable Y, it is a fairly easy task to place the label inside the bar. In Figure 5.5.3a, the value is set with an assignment statement that uses the height of the bar (MEAN) to set the vertical position of the label.

```
y = mean;
```

In order to place the label in the middle of the bar (rather than on top), simply divide the vertical value in half.

```
y = mean/2;
```

Placing text on histograms that have groups

Annotation of histograms that make use of a grouping variable also requires the use of the GROUP variable in the Annotate data set.

In the following example, the imports from each of three countries are grouped within the summer months. Because MONTH is the grouping variable ❷ in the VBAR statement, the GROUP variable in the Annotate data set is created so that it also contains the value of MONTH. ❶

```
proc sort data=annodat.imports
          out=imports;
   by co_code month;
   where month in(6 7 8);
   run;

* Determine the average imports for each month;
proc summary data=imports;
   by co_code month;
   var diamonds;
   output out=mean mean=mean;
   run;

* Create the axis using Annotate;
data anno (keep=xsys ysys function size text angle
               style position
               midpoint group y);
   set mean;
   length function $8;
```

```
      retain xsys ysys '2'  position '3' angle 55
             function 'label'
             size 2 style 'simplex';

      rename co_code=midpoint month=group;  ❶
      y = mean;
      text = left(put(mean,5.2));
run;

axis1 order = (0 to 5 by 1)
      label = (a=90 '$ in Millions');
axis2 label = ('Export Country');
axis3 label = ('Month');

pattern1 v=empty c=red;
pattern2 v=x3    c=red;
pattern3 v=solid c=red;

proc gchart data=mean;
    vbar co_code  / type=mean sumvar=mean
                    anno=anno discrete
                    group=month ❷
                    patternid=midpoint
                    raxis=axis1 maxis=axis2 gaxis=axis3; ❸
    TITLE1 'Summer Diamond Imports for 1945';
    run;
    quit;
```

❶ The variable GROUP contains the value of the month (the grouping variable).

❷ The GROUP= option defines the grouping variable in the VBAR statement.

❸ The GAXIS= option associates the axis statement with the group.

The first four observations in the Annotate data set (WORK.ANNO) are shown next. The code produces Figure 5.5.3b.

OBS	MIDPOINT	GROUP	FUNCTION	XSYS	YSYS	POSITION	ANGLE	SIZE	STYLE	Y	TEXT
1	AZU	6	label	2	2	3	55	2	simplex	3.80	3.80
2	AZU	7	label	2	2	3	55	2	simplex	4.84	4.84
3	AZU	8	label	2	2	3	55	2	simplex	4.33	4.33
4	LIV	6	label	2	2	3	55	2	simplex	2.56	2.56

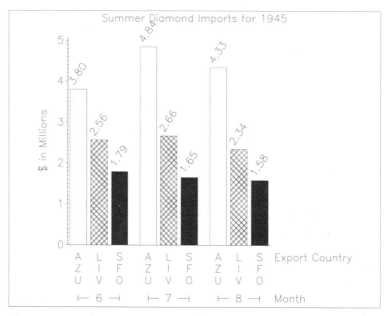

Figure 5.5.3b *Labels placed over grouped histograms require the use of the variables GROUP and MIDPOINT*

More Information

An annotated example of grouped histograms can be found in Horney, 1998.

5.6 Working with GMAPs

The techniques used to add annotated labels to maps produced with PROC GMAP are very similar to those used with PROC GPLOT. Because the maps use X and Y coordinates to locate boundaries and positions within the map, it is possible to use the map information directly to create the Annotate data set.

In the following example, a map of the U.S. southwest is annotated with the name of the state, the name of the state capital, and the number of diamond reselling locations used by Warbucks Industries within that state. Three data sets are used to create the map. The map boundaries are found in MAPS.US, the coordinates for the center point for each state are contained in MAPS.USCENTER ❶, and the coordinates for many of the major cities of the U.S. are contained in MAPS.USCITY ❷.

```
* Create a list of states of interest;
data region;
input stcode $2. state 3. outlets 3.;

label stcode = 'State code'
      state  = 'state number';
datalines;
AZ 4    6   ARIZONA
CA 6   12   CALIFORNIA
CO 8    7   COLORADO
NV 32   5   NEVADA
UT 49   3   UTAH
run;

* Select specific states boundaries;
data usmap(keep=state segment x y);
   merge maps.us region(keep=state in=inreg);
   by state;
   if inreg;
   run;

* Select specific state center points; ❶
data center(keep=state x y stcode outlets);
   merge maps.uscenter
         region(keep=state stcode outlets
                in=inreg);
   by state;
   if inreg;
   run;
```

```
* Select coordinates of the capital cities for;
* each state;
data capital(keep=state city x y); ❷
   merge maps.uscity (where=(capital='Y'))
         region(keep=state in=inreg);
   by state;
   if inreg;
   run;

* Create the Annotate data set;
data anno (keep=xsys ysys function size text when
                style position x y);
   set center(in=incenter)
       capital(in=incapitl);
   length function style $8 text $15;
   retain xsys ysys '2' when 'a' size 2;

   position = '5';
   function = 'label';

   * Label for state center;
   if incenter then do; ❸
      style = 'simplex';
      text = stcode;
      output;
      text = left(put(outlets, 3.)); ❹
      position = '8';
      style = 'centb';
      output;
    end;

   * Label for the state capital;
   if incapitl then do; ❺
      * Place the city name;
      if state in(8,32) then position='2';
      else position = '8';
      style = 'simplex';
      text = city;
      output;

      * Place the city symbol; ❻
      position = '5';
      text = 'M';
      style = 'special';
      output;
   end;
   run;
```

```
proc gmap map=usmap
          data=region;
    id state;
    choro outlets / coutline=black
                    anno=anno  ❼
                    nolegend
                    discrete;
    pattern1 v=empty  c=black r=6;

    title1 'US Southwest';
    title2 'Warbucks Industries';
    title3 'Number of Diamond Resell Locations by State';
    run;
    quit;
```

❸ Using the coordinates of the center of the state, write the two–digit state code.

❹ The number of resell outlets is written below the state code.

❺ The capital name is written below (POSITION='8') the location.

❻ A star (TEXT='M') is placed using the SPECIAL font to designate the capital.

❼ The Annotate data set is selected using the ANNO= option in the CHORO statement.

The data set ANNO, shown here, provides the annotation for the map in Figure 5.6.

OBS	X	Y	FUNCTION	STYLE	TEXT	XSYS	YSYS	WHEN	SIZE	POSITION
1	-0.22318	-0.029980	label	simplex	AZ	2	2	a	2	5
2	-0.22318	-0.029980	label	centb	6	2	2	a	2	8
3	-0.33122	0.037736	label	simplex	CA	2	2	a	2	5
4	-0.33122	0.037736	label	centb	12	2	2	a	2	8
5	-0.13003	0.037180	label	simplex	CO	2	2	a	2	5
6	-0.13003	0.037180	label	centb	7	2	2	a	2	8
7	-0.27722	0.069844	label	simplex	NV	2	2	a	2	5
8	-0.27722	0.069844	label	centb	5	2	2	a	2	8
9	-0.20939	0.053102	label	simplex	UT	2	2	a	2	5
10	-0.20939	0.053102	label	centb	3	2	2	a	2	8
11	-0.23441	-0.046679	label	simplex	Phoenix	2	2	a	2	8
12	-0.23441	-0.046679	label	special	M	2	2	a	2	5
13	-0.34384	0.069866	label	simplex	Sacramento	2	2	a	2	8
14	-0.34384	0.069866	label	special	M	2	2	a	2	5
15	-0.12191	0.049587	label	simplex	Denver	2	2	a	2	2
16	-0.12191	0.049587	label	special	M	2	2	a	2	5
17	-0.31863	0.073757	label	simplex	Carson City	2	2	a	2	2
18	-0.31863	0.073757	label	special	M	2	2	a	2	5
19	-0.21028	0.079145	label	simplex	Salt Lake City	2	2	a	2	8
20	-0.21028	0.079145	label	special	M	2	2	a	2	5

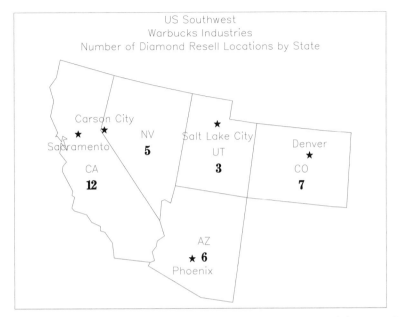

Figure 5.6 *Labels are placed on maps through the use of the X and Y coordinate variables*

More Information

Annotated maps with 'custom-developed blanking' areas for labels are discussed in Bessler, 1997.

Examples of the use of MAPS.USCITY and MAPS.USCENTER to annotate a map can be found in Brown, 1997, and Davis, 1997.

Maps with interior irregular polygons that are built and shaded using Annotate are demonstrated in Hadden, 1997.

CHAPTER 6

Using Annotate Macros as Shortcuts

6.1 Chapter Overview

Annotate macros provide a shortcut when you are using assignment statements to create an Annotate data set. To use these macros properly, you need to understand how they work and what they will do for you. You also need to know how to construct a data set, especially an Annotate data set, before you attempt to use these macros.

6.2 Introduction to Annotate Macros

You can use Annotate macros to simplify the process of creating observations in an Annotate data set. Because macros are executed before the DATA step is compiled and executed, these macros can generate the assignment statements that you would otherwise create yourself.

These macros are predefined to give you the ability to control all of the basic variables associated with any given Annotate function. When controlling a function, the macro name usually assumes the name of the function that is to be defined. Using these macros can eliminate some of the tedium associated with assignment statements.

Unlike the calls to many SAS functions, all arguments to the macros must be specified. Even when you want to use the default value for the argument, the default value must be included (missing values can be used in most cases to achieve the default value). The macro uses the argument to build one or more assignment statements. Very little checking is done by the macro. Consequently, blank or unspecified arguments are more likely to cause errors than to result in the default value for a particular option.

The arguments for the macros may be constants (numbers or character strings), variable names, or literal strings. Consult the documentation in *SAS/GRAPH Software: Reference, Version 6, First Edition* (Vol.1, pp. 570–587) to determine which type is expected for a particular argument. The macro arguments can be one of the following types:

constant   is represented as a number or a quoted string.

variable name   is on the PDV and is **not** quoted.

literal string is placed inside of quotes by the macro and so is not quoted in the macro call. The reference manual indicates which arguments are literals.

When using Annotate macros, remember that the macro call resolves into a series of DATA step assignment statements. Basically, these are the same assignment statements that you could have written if you had chosen not to use the macro. There are two types of Annotate macros: those that prepare or manage the environment and those that define functions.

More Information

This chapter assumes that you have a moderate understanding of SAS macros and how they behave. Additional information on the SAS macro language is available in Carpenter, 1998, and Burlew, 1998.

6.2.1 Macros that prepare the environment

Macros that prepare the environment include

%ANNOMAC   compiles all other Annotate macros and makes them available for use. It is always required.

%DCLANNO   specifies the correct length for all Annotate variables.

%SYSTEM   defines the type of coordinate reference system by assigning values to the variables XSYS, YSYS, and HSYS.

%ANNOMAC

You cannot use Annotate macros unless the %ANNOMAC macro has been called somewhere earlier in the job. This macro compiles all of the remaining Annotate macros, which are then added to the WORK.SASMACR catalog.

%SYSTEM

The syntax for the %SYSTEM macro call is

```
%system(xsys, ysys, hsys)
```

where each argument is a literal and can be 1 through 9 and A, B, or C. These values correspond to the coordinate reference systems described in Sections 2.4 and 5.4.3.

The following section is taken from the SASLOG (with the MPRINT system option on) to show the statements generated by the %SYSTEM macro. The macro requests that the 'Graphics output area - percentage' be used as the basis for the coordinates. Notice that the third argument is not specified and that this results in HSYS being assigned a missing value.

```
182  %system(3,3);
MPRINT(SYSTEM):   XSYS = "3";
MPRINT(SYSTEM):   YSYS = "3";
MPRINT(SYSTEM):   HSYS = "";
```

HSYS is used by several of the macros (such as %LABEL and %SLICE) to determine the units or coordinate system to use when requesting such things as a height for a character or a length of a line. Consult the documentation to determine which macros use HSYS.

6.2.2 Macros that build assignment statements

Macros that create the assignment statements associated with Annotate functions include

%BAR   creates a fillable rectangle.

%CIRCLE   draws an empty circle.

%DRAW   draws a line to a specific point.

%LABEL   writes text at the specified location.

%MOVE   moves to a specific point without drawing.

%POLY   begins drawing a polygon.

%POLYCONT   continues drawing a polygon.

%SLICE   draws a pie slice or an arc.

%LABEL

One of the more complex of these macros is %LABEL. This macro call has nine parameters and, therefore, can replace at least nine assignment statements. %LABEL is illustrated below and more completely in the example in Section 6.3.

The syntax for the %LABEL macro is

```
%label(x,y,text,color,angle,rotate,size,style,position)
```

where

ARGUMENT	TYPE	SPECIFIES....
x & y	number or numeric variable	coordinates for the text string
text	text string or character variable	string to be placed on graphic
color	literal (quotes are not used)	color of the text
angle	number or numeric variable	angle at which to wirte the text
rotate	number or numeric variable	rotation of individual characters of the text
size	number or numeric variable	text size
style	literal	font to be used for the text
position	literal	position of text relative to the X,Y coordinate

The following portion of a SASLOG shows the statements generated by the %LABEL macro:

```
106
%label(50,75,'HomeWanted',blue,.,.,4,script);
MPRINT(LABEL):    X = 50;
MPRINT(LABEL):    Y = 75;
MPRINT(LABEL):    ANGLE = .;
MPRINT(LABEL):    ROTATE = .;
MPRINT(LABEL):    SIZE = 4;
MPRINT(LABEL):    STYLE = "script";
MPRINT(LABEL):    TEXT = 'Home Wanted';
MPRINT(LABEL):    IF "" =: '*' THEN ;
MPRINT(LABEL):    ELSE POSITION = "" ;
MPRINT(LABEL):    IF "blue" =: '*' THEN ;
MPRINT(LABEL):    ELSE COLOR = "blue";
MPRINT(LABEL):    FUNCTION = "LABEL    ";
MPRINT(LABEL):    OUTPUT;
```

In the previous example the last argument of the %LABEL macro call (position) is left blank. An examination of the code (**in bold**) shows that this did not result in an error for this argument. However, as a general rule, it is not wise to leave arguments blank.

More Information
Kenny, 1994, includes several examples of Annotate macros.
Both Griffin, 1995, and Claude, 1997, include examples that use the %LABEL macro and include some discussion of %ANNOMAC.
Nyberg, 1994, has Annotate macro examples that include the use of %DRAW, %MOVE, %BAR, and %LABEL.

6.3 Classified Ad Revisited

In Section 4.2 the example creates three labels through a series of assignment statements. The same code is used below; however, the assignment statements have been commented out and replaced with calls to Annotate macros. The commented code has been left in the DATA step for demonstration purposes. The first Annotate macro called must be %ANNOMAC.

```
%annomac

* USE PROC GSLIDE AND ANNOTATE TO CREATE A CLASSIFIED;
* AD FOR ANNIE.;
DATA ANNIE;
    LENGTH FUNCTION COLOR STYLE $8;

    *RETAIN XSYS YSYS '5';
    %system(5,5)

    *RETAIN FUNCTION 'LABEL' X 50;
    *COLOR='BLUE';
    *STYLE='SCRIPT';
    *SIZE=4;
    *TEXT='Home Wanted        ';  ❶
    *X=50;
    *Y=75;
    *OUTPUT;
    %label(50,75,'Home Wanted    ❶   ',blue,0,0,4,script);
```

```
*SIZE=2;
    *Y=50;
    *STYLE='DUPLEX';
    *TEXT='GIRL - WITHOUT EYES';
    *OUTPUT;
    %label(50,50,'GIRL - WITHOUT EYES',*,0,0,2,duplex);

    *Y=30;
    *STYLE='TRIPLEX';
    *COLOR='GREEN';
    *TEXT='Has Dog / Will Travel';
    *OUTPUT;
    %label(50,30,'Has Dog / Will Travel',green,0,0,2,triplex);
run;

PROC GSLIDE ANNO=ANNIE;
    TITLE1 F=SWISS H=3 'Classified Ad';
run;
quit;
```

When the commented code is removed from the DATA step, the code becomes

```
* USE PROC GSLIDE AND ANNOTATE TO CREATE A CLASSIFIED;
* AD FOR ANNIE.;
DATA ANNIE;
    LENGTH FUNCTION COLOR STYLE $8;
    %system(5,5)
    %label(50,75,'Home Wanted             ',blue,0,0,4,script);
    %label(50,50,'GIRL - WITHOUT EYES',*,0,0,2,duplex);
    %label(50,30,'Has Dog / Will
Travel',green,0,0,2,triplex);
run;
```

❶The length of the TEXT variable is set in the first %LABEL by padding the string with blanks. It is generally smarter to use a LENGTH statement.

Although the new program is much shorter (fewer statements) than the one used in Section 4.2, it is not more efficient. We are now using the %SYSTEM macro to assign the values to XSYS and YSYS when the RETAIN statement would be quicker.

The macros create and assign values to a number of variables that are not needed and should be dropped. These include HSYS, POSITION, ANGLE, and ROTATE. Some of these variables can be eliminated by using an asterisk (*) as the parameter value.

The data set ANNIE contains the following three observations:

OBS	FUNCTION	COLOR	STYLE	XSYS	YSYS	HSYS
1	LABEL	blue	script	5	5	
2	LABEL	blue	duplex	5	5	
3	LABEL	green	triplex	5	5	

OBS	X	Y	ANGLE	ROTATE	SIZE	TEXT	POSITION
1	50	75	0	0	4	Home Wanted	
2	50	50	0	0	2	GIRL-WITHOUT EYES	
3	50	30	0	0	2	Has Dog/Will Travel	

Figure 6.3 *Annotate macros can be used as assignment statement coding shortcuts*

More Information

This and other examples using various Annotate macros are shown in Carpenter, 1999.

Pakalniskis, 1999, uses Annotate macros to modify bubble plots.

References

SAS Institute Documentation

SAS Institute Inc. SAS Online Doc, Version 8, Cary, NC: SAS Institute Inc., 1999.

SAS Institute Inc. (1990), *SAS/GRAPH Software: Reference, Version 6, First Edition, 2 volumes,* Cary, NC: SAS Institute Inc.

SAS Institute Inc. (1991), *SAS/GRAPH Software: Usage, Version 6, First Edition.* Cary, NC: SAS Institute Inc.

Articles, Papers and Books

Bessler, LeRoy (1997), "Map Smart: Design and Build Effective InfoGeographics Using PROC GMAP and Software Intelligence," in *Proceedings of the Twentieth Annual SUGI Conference.* Cary, NC: SAS Institute Inc., 775–784.

Brown, Keith J. (1997), "PROC GMAP: How I Learned to Tolerate (And Almost Love) Annotating," in *Proceedings of the Twentieth Annual SUGI Conference.* Cary, NC: SAS Institute Inc., 769–774.

Burlew, Michele M. (1998), *SAS Macro Programming Made Easy*. Cary, NC: SAS Institute Inc. 280 pp.

Carpenter, Arthur L. (1988), "Horizontal Contour Lines Using the G3D Procedure," in *Proceedings of the Thirteenth Annual SUGI Conference*. Cary, NC: SAS Institute Inc., 382–386.

Carpenter, Arthur L. (1991), "Marie Annotate: How Not to Lose Your Head When Enhancing SAS/GRAPH Output," in *Proceedings of the Sixteenth Annual SUGI Conference*. Cary, NC: SAS Institute Inc., 743–747.

Carpenter, Arthur L. (1992), "Little Orphan Annotate: How to Dress Up SAS/GRAPH Output," in *Proceedings of the Seventeenth Annual SUGI Conference*. Cary, NC: SAS Institute Inc., 549–554.

Carpenter, Arthur L. (1994), "The ANNOTATE Facility: A Quick Start to an Easy Overview," in *Proceedings of the Nineteenth Annual SUGI Conference*. Cary, NC: SAS Institute Inc., 1423–1428.

Carpenter, Arthur L. (1998), *Carpenter's Complete Guide to the SAS Macro Language*. Cary, NC: SAS Institute Inc. 242 pp.

Carpenter, Arthur L. (1999), "Using ANNOTATE Macros As Shortcuts," in *Proceedings of the Twenty-Fourth Annual SUGI Conference*. Cary, NC: SAS Institute Inc., 1006–1011.

Chinn, Bruce (1997), "Effectively Displaying Statistical Results in a High Volume Drug Research Environment Using SAS/GRAPH," in *Proceedings of the Twenty-Second Annual SUGI Conference.* Cary, NC: SAS Institute Inc., 819–823.

Claude, Kathy and Joseph Guido (1997), "Enhanced Shewhart Plots Using Graphics Template and Annotation," in *Proceedings of the Twenty-Second Annual SUGI Conference.* Cary, NC: SAS Institute Inc. 1073–1076.

Davis, Michael (1997), "Putting Yourself on the Map with the GMAP Procedure," in *Proceedings of the Twenty-Second Annual SUGI Conference.* Cary, NC: SAS Institute Inc., 274–283.

Dorr, David and Mae Gordon (1998), "Graphically Conquering the SF-36: A Tool for Illustrating Subscale by Group Over Time Using SAS/GRAPH Software," in *Proceedings of the Twenty-Third Annual SUGI Conference.* Cary, NC: SAS Institute Inc., 856–860.

Elkin, Steven E., William Mietlowski, Kevin McCague, and Andrea Kay (1997), "Creating Complex Graphics for Survival Analyses with the SAS System," in *Proceedings of the Twenty-Second Annual SUGI Conference.* Cary, NC: SAS Institute Inc., 824–829.

Gilbert, Jeffery D. (1999), "Customizing SAS Graphs Using the Annotate Facility and Global Statements," in *Proceedings of the Twenty-Fourth Annual SUGI Conference.* Cary, NC: SAS Institute Inc., 1002–1005.

Griffin, Lori (1995), "When Graphing Anything is Possible: Once you know how to ANNOTATE (Tips and techniques to make using Annotate more effective and easier to use)," in *Proceedings of the Twentieth Annual SUGI Conference*. Cary, NC: SAS Institute Inc., 1064–1069.

Griffin, Lori (1997), "Graphing: Taking the Mystery Out of Subscripts and Superscripts (The Why Not's and How To's Are Presented)," in *Proceedings of the Twenty-Second Annual SUGI Conference*. Cary, NC: SAS Institute Inc., 800–806.

Hadden, Louise, Mike Murphy, and Alan J. White (1997), "From 50,000,000 Claims to One Analytical File," in *Proceedings of the Twenty-Second Annual SUGI Conference*. Cary, NC: SAS Institute Inc., 964–969.

Horney, Anne and Gail F. Kirk. (1998), "One Bar Chart, Two Variables, Three Axes," in *Proceedings of the Twenty-Third Annual SUGI Conference*. Cary, NC: SAS Institute Inc., 1086–1090.

Kenny, Susan J. (1994), "Integrating Statistical Information into Graphical Displays," in *Proceedings of the Nineteenth Annual SUGI Conference*. Cary, NC: SAS Institute Inc., 740–749.

Kenny, Susan J. (1998), "How Not To Hate ANNOTATE," in *Proceedings of the Twenty-Third Annual SUGI Conference*. Cary, NC: SAS Institute Inc., 845–851.

Kirk, Gail F. and Anne Horney (1998), "Exploring Multi-dimensional Relationships with SAS/GRAPH Software," in *Proceedings of the Twenty-Third Annual SUGI Conference.* Cary, NC: SAS Institute Inc., 1100–1105.

Mendelson, Irene (1996), "SAS/GRAPH Software: Doing More with Less ANNOTATE," in *Proceedings of the Twenty-First Annual SUGI Conference.* Cary, NC: SAS Institute Inc., 280–285.

Nyberg, Jack S. and Stuart D. Nichols (1994), "SAS/GRAPH: Using the Annotate Facility," in *Proceedings of the Nineteenth Annual SUGI Conference.* Cary, NC: SAS Institute Inc., 721–725.

Pakalniskis, Alexander, Alein Chum, Gail P. Grant, and Bruce Davidson (1999), "Using SAS/GRAPH To Compare Physician Practice," in *Proceedings of the Twenty-Fourth Annual SUGI Conference.* Cary, NC: SAS Institute Inc., 1437–1442.

Pratter, Frederick (1997), "Graphical Solutions for Market Intelligence," in *Proceedings of the Twenty-Second Annual SUGI Conference.* Cary, NC: SAS Institute Inc., 848–855.

Vierkant, Robert A. (1998), "Creating Scatterplot Matrices Using SAS/GRAPH Software," in *Proceedings of the Twenty-Third Annual SUGI Conference.* Cary, NC: SAS Institute Inc., 821–826.

Appendix - Data

ANNODAT.IMPORTS

```
*************************************************;
* imports.sas
*
* Create the Warbucks import data set for 1945;
*************************************************;

data annodat.imports;
input @1   diamonds
      @6   gold
      @11  silver
      @34  DATE
      @40  co_code $3.
      @44  MONTH
    ;
* Adjust the year value;
* Change from 1988 to 1945;
date = mdy(month(date), day(date), 1945);
format date date7.;
datalines;
1.58 1.35 10.96 3.18 54.9   59.5   10241 AZU 1
2.77 1.25 12.73 2.96 60.2   58.5   10272 AZU 2
3.59 1.26 15.5  6.11 62.8   58     10301 AZU 3
3.48 1.05 15.01 4.69 63.4   72.75  10332 AZU 4
4.53 0.95 19.69 6.06 67.6   70     10362 AZU 5
3.8  0.93 17.48 7.68 69     74.75  10393 AZU 6
4.84 0.97 19.32 9.41 76.5   79.5   10423 AZU 7
4.33 1.3  18.06 8.84 74.5   78.75  10454 AZU 8
3.95 1.46 17.36 7.95 72.9   75.75  10485 AZU 9
3.18 1.76 22.81 8.93 70.1   76.25  10515 AZU 10
2.18 1.71 14.22 5.59 60     70.75  10546 AZU 11
1.9  0.99 8.7   2.58 54.6   56.5   10576 AZU 12
0.78 1.36 5     2.78 51.9   .      10241 LIV 1
0.89 1.28 8.13  3.7  56.5   .      10272 LIV 2
1.64 0.98 3.58  3.63 59.1   .      10301 LIV 3
2.89 0.94 3.28  3.28 59     .      10332 LIV 4
2.75 0.89 2.6   2.6  59.9   .      10362 LIV 5
2.56 0.84 2.95  2.71 62.7   .      10393 LIV 6
2.66 0.88 3.74  3.72 65.1   .      10423 LIV 7
2.34 0.88 4.63  3.59 65.41  .      10454 LIV 8
2.7  1.06 4.18  3.9  62.1   .      10485 LIV 9
1.88 1.14 6.03  3.99 59.6   .      10515 LIV 10
1.31 1.08 1.94  2.38 54.5   .      10546 LIV 11
1.28 1.45 4.85  2.38 49.8   .      10576 LIV 12
1.28 2.44 4.34  4.25 50.6   77.75  10241 SFO 1
1.38 2.58 4.6   5.98 54.5   70.75  10272 SFO 2
1.6  2.05 1.56  4.83 56.5   68     10301 SFO 3
```

```
2.39 1.76 1.93  4.84 58.1  68     10332 SFO 4
2.35 1.58 1.82  3.5  59.5  69.5   10362 SFO 5
1.79 1.6  1.2   4.11 62.5  70     10393 SFO 6
1.65 1.85 4.25  4.31 65.3  72.75  10423 SFO 7
1.58 1.64 1.84  4.63 65    72.75  10454 SFO 8
1.83 2.01 3.08  5.03 63.1  75.25  10485 SFO 9
1.62 2.14 1.81  4.58 61.4  80.25  10515 SFO 10
1.43 2.02 1.33  4.11 56.5  78     10546 SFO 11
0.9  2.21 8.23  6.33 50.4  74.75  10576 SFO 12
;
```

Index

Call your local SAS office to order these books from Books by Users Press

Advanced Log-Linear Models Using SAS®
by **Daniel Zelterman** . . . . .Order No. A57496

Annotate: Simply the Basics
by **Art Carpenter** . . . . .Order No. A57320

Applied Multivariate Statistics with SAS® Software,
Second Edition
by **Ravindra Khattree**
and **Dayanand N. Naik** . . . . .Order No. A56903

Applied Statistics and the SAS® Programming
Language, Fourth Edition
by **Ronald P. Cody**
and **Jeffrey K. Smith** . . . . .Order No. A55984

An Array of Challenges — Test Your SAS® Skills
by **Robert Virgile** . . . . .Order No. A55625

Beyond the Obvious with SAS® Screen Control
Language
by **Don Stanley** . . . . .Order No. A55073

Carpenter's Complete Guide to the SAS® Macro
Language
by **Art Carpenter** . . . . .Order No. A56100

The Cartoon Guide to Statistics
by **Larry Gonick**
and **Woollcott Smith** . . . . .Order No. A5515

Categorical Data Analysis Using the SAS® System,
Second Edition
by **Maura E. Stokes, Charles S. Davis,**
and **Gary G. Koch** . . . . .Order No. A57998

Client/Server Survival Guide, Third Edition
by **Robert Orfali, Dan Harkey,**
and **Jeri Edwards** . . . . .Order No. A58099

Cody's Data Cleaning Techniques Using SAS® Software
by **Ron Cody** .Order No. A57198

Common Statistical Methods for Clinical Research
with SAS® Examples, Second Edition
by **Glenn A. Walker** . . . . .Order No. A58086

Concepts and Case Studies in Data Management
by **William S. Calvert**
and **J. Meimei Ma** . . . . .Order No. A55220

Debugging SAS® Programs: A Handbook of Tools
and Techniques
by **Michele M. Burlew** . . . . .Order No. A57743

Efficiency: Improving the Performance of Your SAS®
Applications
by **Robert Virgile** . . . . .Order No. A55960

A Handbook of Statistical Analyses Using SAS®,
Second Edition
by **B.S. Everitt**
and **G. Der** . . . . .Order No. A58679

Health Care Data and the SAS® System
by **Marge Scerbo, Craig Dickstein,**
and **Alan Wilson** . . . . .Order No. A57638

The How-To Book for SAS/GRAPH® Software
by **Thomas Miron** . . . . .Order No. A55203

support.sas.com/pubs

Strategic Data Warehousing Principles Using
SAS® Software
by **Peter R. Welbrock** . . . . .Order No. A56278

Survival Analysis Using the SAS® System:
A Practical Guide
by **Paul D. Allison** . . . . .Order No. A55233

Table-Driven Strategies for Rapid SAS® Applications
Development
by **Tanya Kolosova**
and **Samuel Berestizhevsky** . . . . . . .Order No. A55198

Tuning SAS® Applications in the MVS Environment
by **Michael A. Raithel** . . . . .Order No. A55231

Univariate and Multivariate General Linear Models:
Theory and Applications Using SAS® Software
by **Neil H. Timm**
and **Tammy A. Mieczkowski** . . . . . . .Order No. A55809

Using SAS® in Financial Research
by **Ekkehart Boehmer, John Paul Broussard,**
and **Juha-Pekka Kallunki** . . . . .Order No. A57601

Using the SAS® Windowing Environment:
A Quike Tutorial
by **Larry Hatcher** . . . . .Order No. A57201

Visualizing Categorical Data
by **Michael Friendly** . . . . .Order No. A56571

Working with the SAS® System
by **Erik W. Tilanus** . . . . .Order No. A55190

Your Guide to Survey Research Using the
SAS® System
by **Archer Gravely** . . . . .Order No. A55688

JMP® Books

Basic Business Statistics: A Casebook
by **Dean P. Foster, Robert A. Stine,**
and **Richard P. Waterman** . . . . .Order No. A56813

Business Analysis Using Regression: A Casebook
by **Dean P. Foster, Robert A. Stine,**
and **Richard P. Waterman** . . . . .Order No. A56818

JMP® Start Statistics, Second Edition
by **John Sall, Ann Lehman,**
and **Lee Creighton** . . . . .Order No. A58166

Regression Using JMP®
by **Rudolf J. Freund, Ramon C. Littell,**
and **Lee Creighton** . . . . .Order No. A58789

support.sas.com/pubs

Welcome * Bienvenue *Willkommen *Yohkoso * Bienvenido

SAS Publishing Is Easy to Reach

Visit our Web site located at support.sas.com/pubs

You will find product and service details, including

- **companion Web sites**
- **sample chapters**
- **tables of contents**
- **author biographies**
- **book reviews**

Learn about

- **regional users group conferences**
- **trade show sites and dates**
- **authoring opportunities**
- **e-books**

Explore all the services that Publications has to offer!

Your Listserv Subscription Automatically Brings the News to You

Do you want to be among the first to learn about the latest books and services available from SAS Publishing? Subscribe to our listserv **newdocnews-l** and, once each month, you will automatically receive a description of the newest books and which environments or operating systems and SAS® release(s) each book addresses.

To subscribe,

1. Send an e-mail message to **listserv@vm.sas.com**.

2. Leave the "Subject" line blank.

3. Use the following text for your message:

   subscribe NEWDOCNEWS-L *your-first-name your-last-name*

   For example: subscribe NEWDOCNEWS-L John Doe

You're Invited to Publish with SAS Institute's Books by Users Press

If you enjoy writing about SAS software and how to use it, the Books by Users program at SAS Institute offers a variety of publishing options. We are actively recruiting authors to publish books and sample code.

If you find the idea of writing a book by yourself a little intimidating, consider writing with a co-author. Keep in mind that you will receive complete editorial and publishing support, access to our users, technical advice and assistance, and competitive royalties. Please ask us for an author packet at **sasbbu@sas.com** or call 919-531-7447. See the Books by Users Web page at **support.sas.com/bbu** for complete information.

Book Discount Offered at SAS Public Training Courses!

When you attend one of our SAS Public Training Courses at any of our regional Training Centers in the United States, you will receive a 20% discount on any book orders placed during the course. Take advantage of this offer at the next course you attend!

SAS Institute Inc.
SAS Campus Drive
Cary, NC 27513-2414
Fax 919-677-4444

E-mail: sasbook@sas.com
Web page: support.sas.com/pubs
To order books, call SAS Publishing Sales at 800-727-3228*
For product information, consulting, customer service, or training, call 800-727-0025
For other SAS Institute business, call 919-677-8000*

* Note: Customers outside the United States should contact their local SAS office.

The Power to Know.

SAS Publishing